LEONARD DRUMSET METHOD

BY KENNAN WYLIE

...ES AUDIO & VIDEO!

CONTENTS

PLAYBACK+
Speed • Pitch • Balance • Loop

To access audio, video, and extra content visit:
www.halleonard.com/mylibrary

Enter Code
3912-4947-0709-2228

ISBN 978-1-4950-8333-4

HAL•LEONARD®

7777 W. BLUEMOUND RD. P.O. BOX 13819 MILWAUKEE, WI 53213

▶ INTRODUCTION

Book 2 of the *Hal Leonard Drumset Method* is designed to help the beginning drummer explore four-limb independence through the use of ostinato patterns, syncopated grooves, fills, and beat combination patterns. Basic chart reading will be covered, including articulations, musical symbols, and ensemble figures, along with brush playing and even how to build a basic drum solo. Musical styles such as funk, country, hip-hop, soca, Afro-Cuban, Brazilian, and more are also introduced. Like Book 1, this comprehensive method also includes audio demonstration and play-along tracks, plus video lessons.

ABOUT THE AUDIO AND VIDEO

To access the audio and video files that accompany this book, simply visit **www.halleonard.com/mylibrary** and enter the code found on page 1. From here you can download or stream all of the audio and video files.

Each main exercise and song in this book includes two audio tracks:

1. A **demonstration track** that includes the notated drum part so you can hear how the example is supposed to sound.

2. A **play-along track** of the same example *without* the drums, so you can practice it along with the backing instruments.

The audio tracks for each exercise continue on a loop for approximately three minutes so you have plenty of time to listen or play along. When there are multiple lines within one exercise, the band will continue playing through them without any breaks.

Video lessons are also included, featuring drum master Gregg Bissonette! Gregg will demonstrate introductory concepts, song examples, and techniques throughout the book.

Examples including audio and/or video are marked with icons throughout:

ABOUT THE DOWNLOADABLE PDF

In addition to the audio and video, you also have access to even more content: a downloadable PDF containing further drum exercises for study and practice. You can download the PDF using the same access code and website mentioned above.

HOW TO PRACTICE

1. **Go Slowly:** Learn new beats and stickings at a slow tempo.

2. **Use a Metronome:** Always use a metronome to reinforce good time-keeping.

3. **Be Repetitive:** Each line should be repeated up to 10 times, at a minimum, to develop muscle memory.

4. **Stay Relaxed:** Avoid tension in the grip, the feet, and the body.

5. **Record Yourself:** Record yourself playing and self-evaluate what you hear.

LESSON 1: LIMB INDEPENDENCE

QUICK TIP – When practicing different ostinato patterns, try to be aware of the notes that land within the 8th-note pulse. A solid groove depends on the consistent placement of these notes.

A common way to take a simple beat and transform it into another variation is by changing the ostinato pattern in the right hand. An **ostinato** pattern is a musical figure that is repetitive. For instance, the right hand usually plays 8th or 16th notes on the hi-hat or ride cymbal. Here is an example of taking a basic groove and changing the ostinato pattern. Keep in mind that these are just a few variations. Use your creativity to come up with patterns you like.

Ostinato Exercise

After you have mastered all of these different ostinato patterns with the right hand, try reversing the hands. Play the hi-hat ostinato with the left hand and the snare drum with the right hand. Take your time and practice slowly.

Independence Exercise

Four-limb independence can be practiced by adding left foot (stepping) hi-hat rhythms to the ostinato patterns. Play the following beats with the previous ostinato patterns, this time adding the left-foot ostinato patterns shown below (A–D) on the hi-hat. **Note:** on the audio demonstration track, only the A and C left-foot ostinato patterns are played.

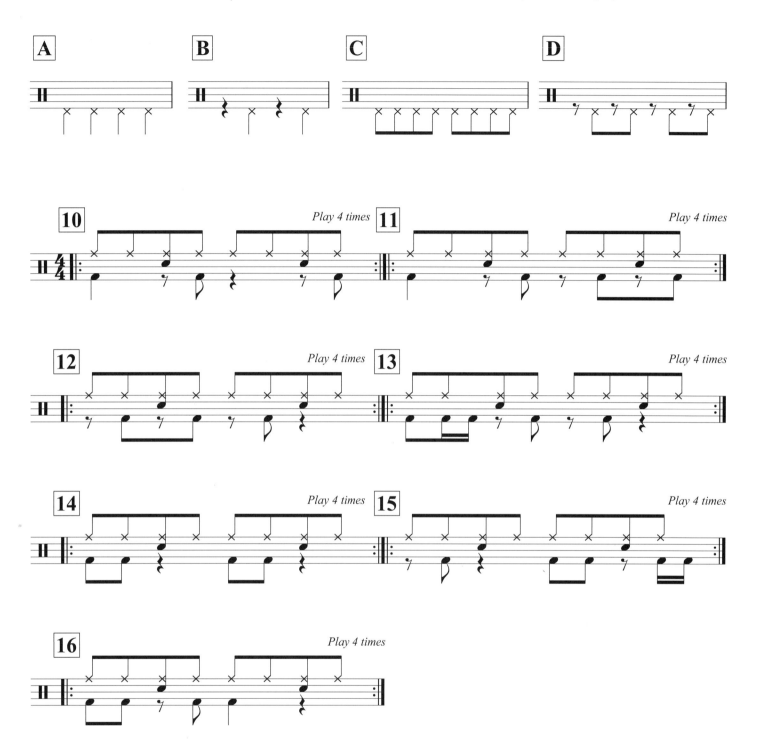

LESSON 2: HALF-TIME GROOVES

> **QUICK TIP** – Be careful to visualize the music on the chart when playing in half-time. Since the backbeat occurs only on beat 3, the music tends to flow a bit faster from measure to measure.

Half-time feel is another type of groove that every drummer should know well. This occurs when the usual backbeat on beats 2 and 4 shifts to beat 3 instead. It gives the music a totally different feel even though the tempo has not changed. Many drummers tend to rush the tempo when playing half-time because there is more space between the backbeats. It is very important to hear all of the subdivisions in your head. Let's try a few half-time grooves:

Half-Time Grooves

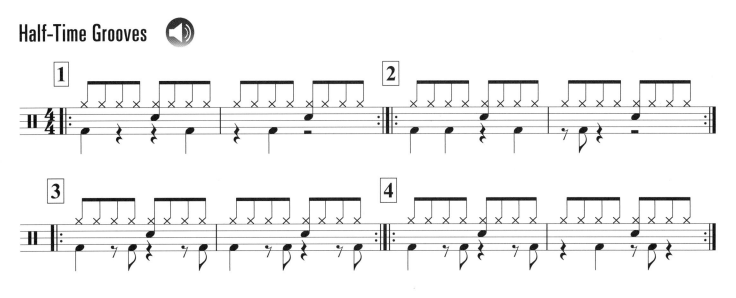

Half-Time Transitions

The next step is "entering" and "exiting" the half-time groove from the original groove. The use of a simple fill can help bridge these two grooves. At first this may present some coordination issues, but they can easily be resolved by repetition. Try using any of the previous half-time grooves in the B section of the following example.

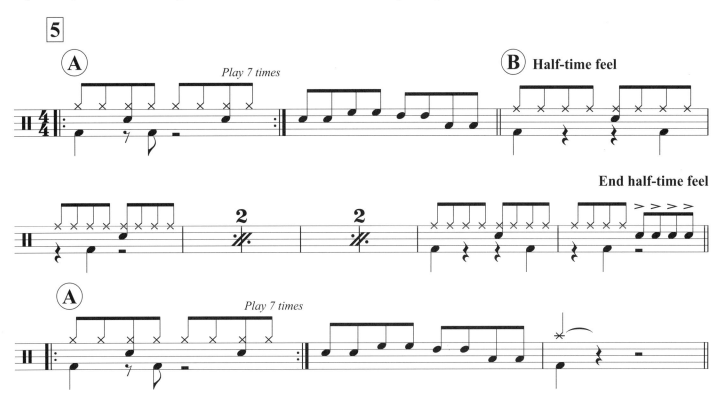

"HALFWAY HOME"

Here is a funk groove that moves into a half-time feel.

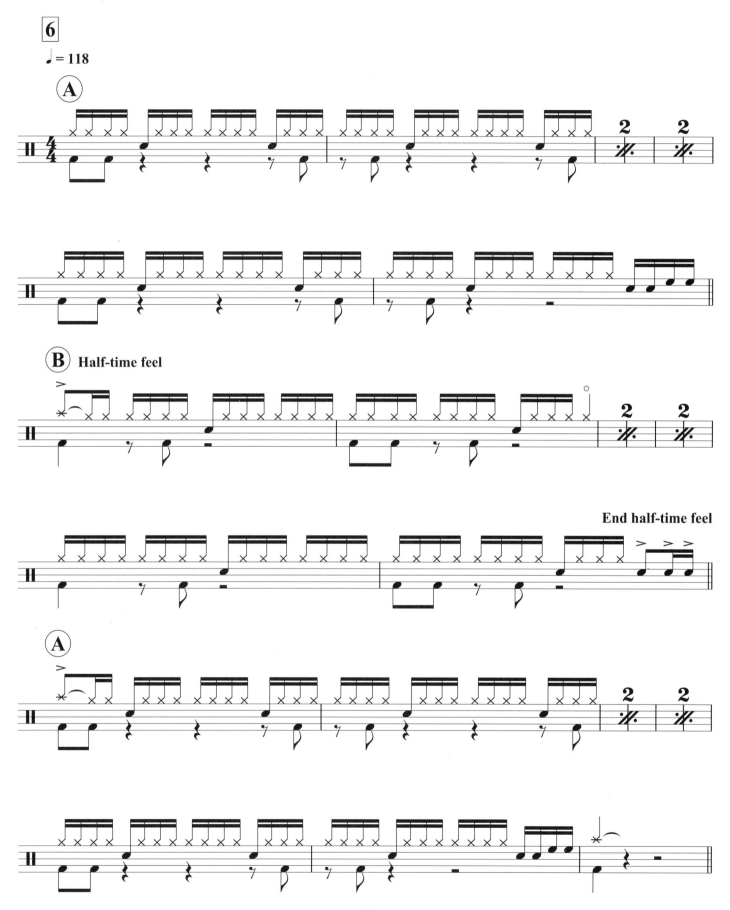

6

"SIDEWALK SHUFFLE"

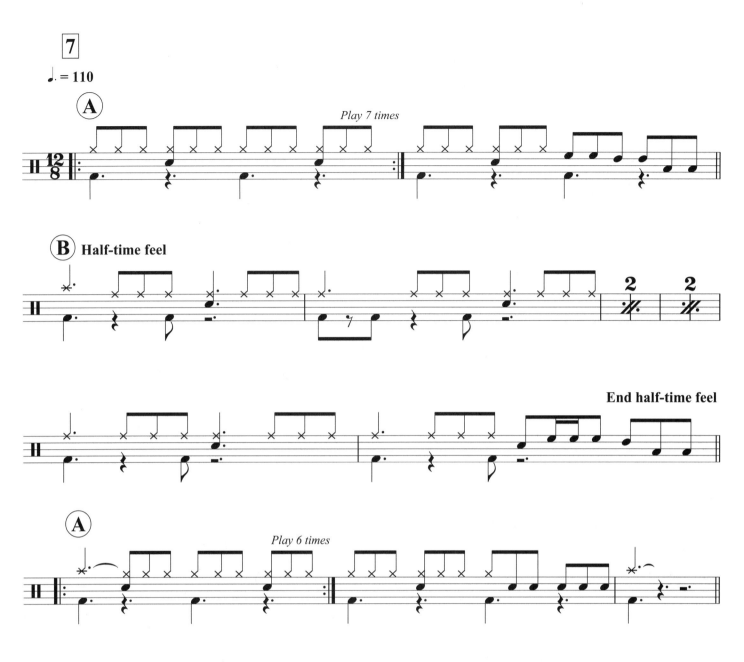

LESSON 3: 16TH RESTS

The 16th rest (𝄾) can create many interesting syncopated rhythms. Check out the rhythms that are made as we move the 16th rest around to different parts of the beat.

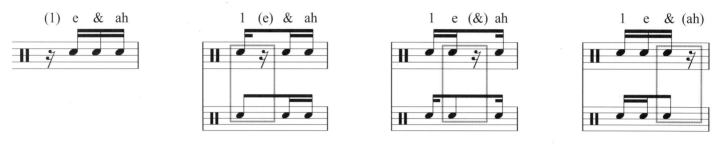

Combining three 16th notes can create one dotted 8th note (♪.) or one dotted 8th rest (𝄾.):

New Rhythms Exercise 🔊

Try the following lines with some of these new rhythms. Notice that the written stickings are derived from a "flow sticking system," where each leading group of four 16ths starts with the right hand.

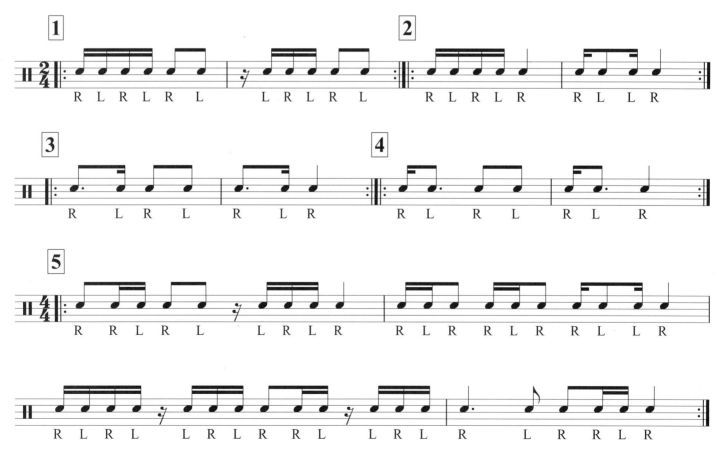

8

6

R R L R L R L R   R R L R L R L R

R L R L   L R R L   L   R R L R L R L R

Bass and Snare Groove Variations

Following are patterns that make use of some of our newest 16th rhythms. The "A" examples will use an alternating 16th-note pattern on the hi-hat, while the "B" examples contain an 8th-note pattern on the ride cymbal (or hi-hat, if you prefer). Notice how the bass drum lines up with the hand subdivision. **Note:** on the audio demonstration track, only the "A" examples are played.

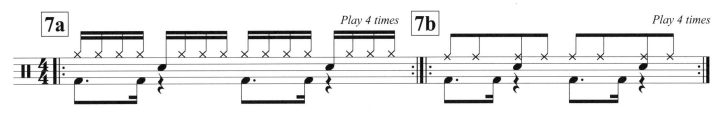

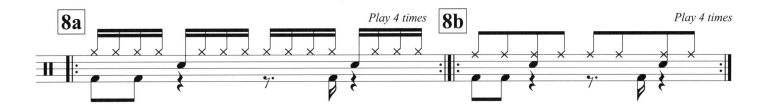

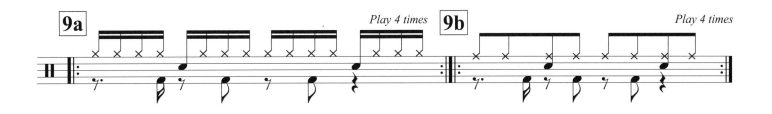

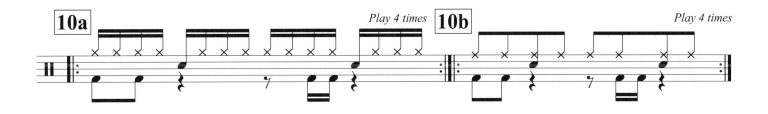

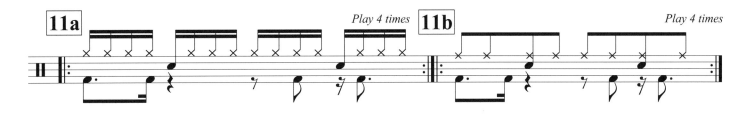

"POCKET CHANGE"

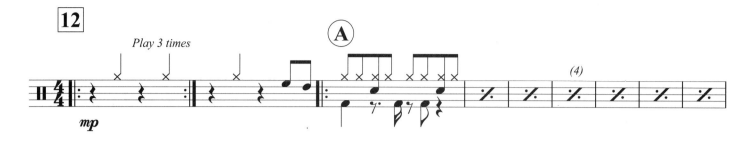

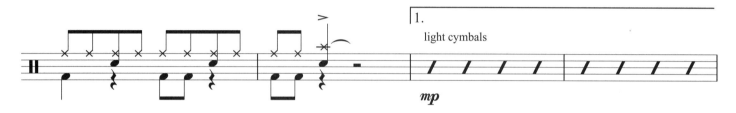

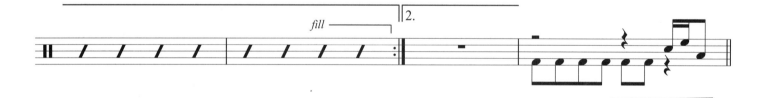

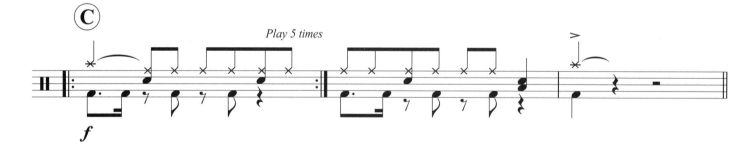

10

LESSON 4: SYNCOPATED FILLS

QUICK TIP – In funk music, drum fills tend to be shorter in length because the music is very groove-oriented.

With knowledge of 8th- and 16th-note rhythms, fills with more syncopation can now be used. This will give the drummer many more creative ideas for adding rhythmical interest. Here are some examples:

Two-Beat Fills

One-Bar Fills

Syncopated Grooves

Adding an extra snare drum note to the existing backbeats can make some grooves even more funky!

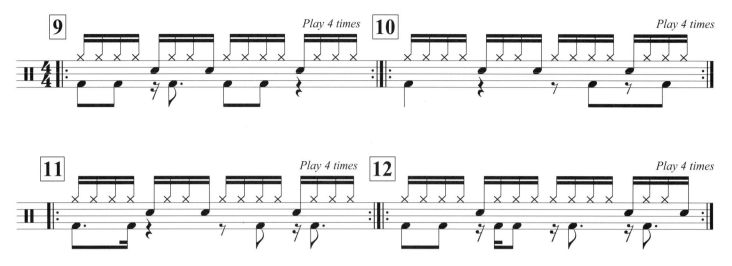

 "PHAT MONKEY"

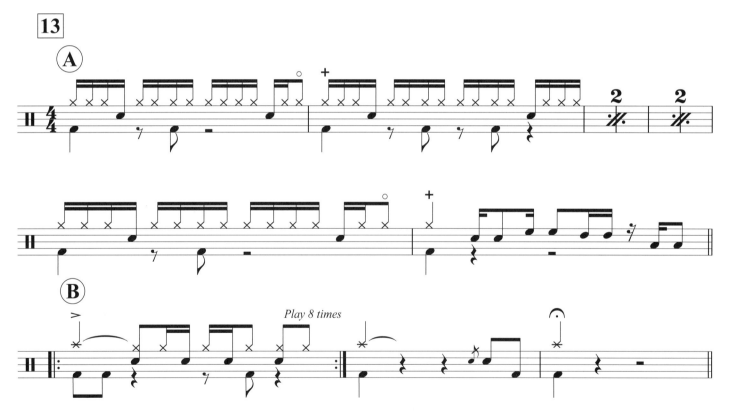

LESSON 5: FUNK GROOVES

QUICK TIP – Opening the hi-hat during a 16th-note groove is a great way to break up the beat. It starts to sound funky because of the moving 16th-note accents.

Playing 16th-note grooves with the right hand as the ostinato can become challenging if the player does not have adequate technique. A basic technical foundation is necessary for these grooves to be played. Remember to slow the tempo down accordingly and use a relaxed stroke. Try some of these funk grooves.

Funk Grooves

Note: on the audio demonstration track, only the "A" examples are played.

Opening the hi-hat within right-handed 16th-note grooves can really add some variety to the beat. Remember to space the hi-hat cymbals apart enough so the open sound can be audible. The tempo and rhythm will most likely determine if you should use the "heel-toe" technique or the "bounce" technique. Here are some basic hi-hat variations you can practice with the simple groove listed below them. Open and close the hi-hat in tempo.

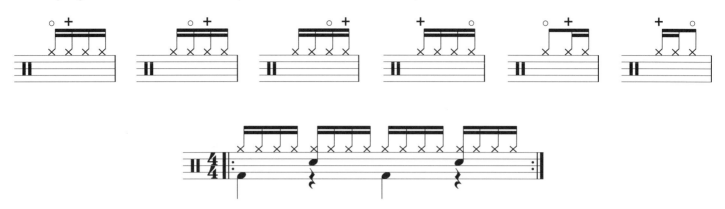

Hi-Hat Variations

Now try these grooves with some hi-hat variations.

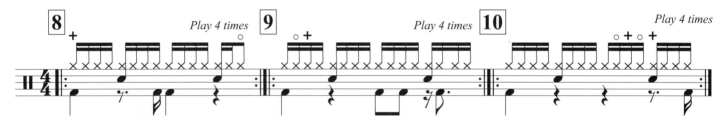

"SHARE MY GROOVE"

14

LESSON 6: DISPLACED BACKBEATS

In the 1970s, funk and rock started to merge together, creating a new spread of syncopated grooves. These types of grooves commonly used shifting accents to give the music a fresh sound. Typically, the snare drum is played on beats 2 and 4 (the backbeats), but during this time period, the snare drum began to be "displaced" to other beats. Here are some examples of this.

Displaced Snare Grooves

Note: on the audio demonstration track, the "A" examples (ride cymbal grooves) are played through first, followed by the "B" examples (hi-hat grooves).

Some of the most influential leaders of this "greasy" groove were the drummers for the James Brown Band. Here's a look at one of the most popular grooves:

"HOT SWEAT"

TIME TO GET FUNKY

Any drummer can get funky and create some beat combinations with the 16th-note syncopated rhythms you have learned. Use any mixture of examples 6–20 below with one or more "beat 2 and 4" combos from A–E. You can come up with hundreds of beats.

Funky Combos

The audio demonstration features different combinations of the following one-beat rhythms. The full example shown below them is a sample combination of these.

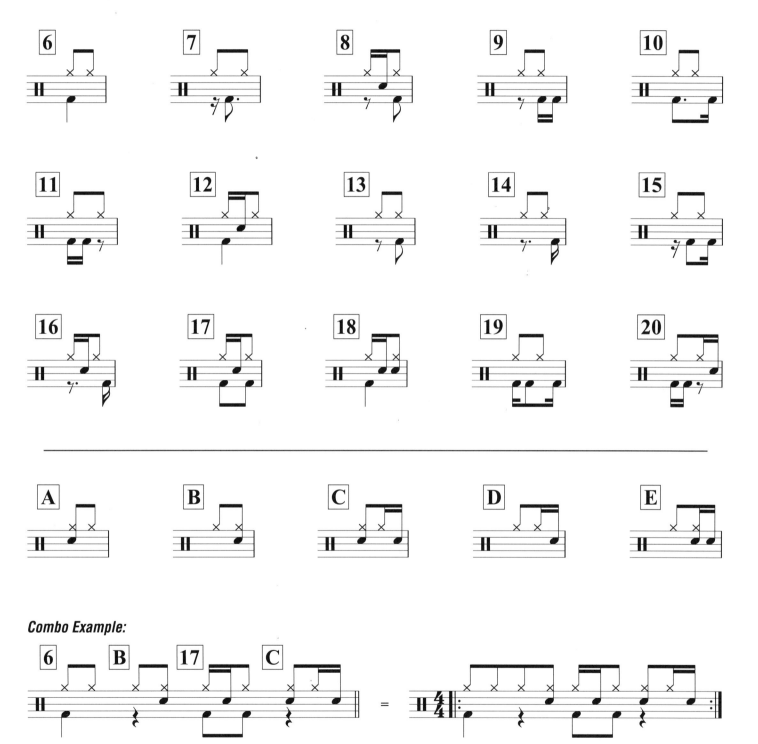

Combo Example:

Rimshot – played by striking the drumhead and rim at the same time. This technique is used very often for playing the backbeats in certain styles of music. It is notated with an "X" notehead.

 "BRING ME THERE"

This tune includes cross-stick and rimshots.

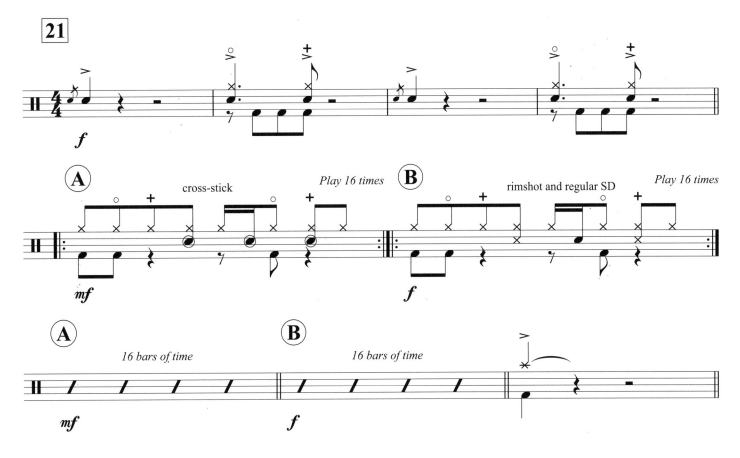

LESSON 7: GHOST NOTES

> **QUICK TIP** – Some of the most notable masters of ghost-note drumming include Harvey Mason, Bernard Purdie, Steve Gadd, and David Garibaldi.

UNDERSTANDING GHOST NOTES

Ghost notes are a very big part of funk and R&B music (rhythm and blues). The term "ghosted" refers to notes played but not always heard. In other words, they are a bit softer compared to the main notes or accents. Using ghost notes can really give your drumming a special feel and unique quality. They are played at a lighter volume level with a lower stick height, similar to playing unaccented taps. Playing the unaccented notes lower really gives this style of music its character; they are more "felt" than heard. In order to play ghost notes, you will need a proficient level of control to execute unaccented notes directly after an accent. Try the following sticking on a single surface and then move the right-hand accents around the drums while keeping the other notes low.

$$\overset{>}{R}\ L\ \overset{>}{R}\ L\ L\ \overset{>}{R}\ L\ L$$

Also try paradiddle sticking:

$$\overset{>}{R}\ L\ R\ R\ \overset{>}{L}\ R\ L\ L$$

In this chapter we will help identify the ghosted notes by placing them in parentheses. Remember to make a nice contrast between the accented notes and unaccented notes.

Ghost-Note Exercise

Try a few hands-only grooves that contain a few more ghosted notes.

Ghost Hands Exercise 1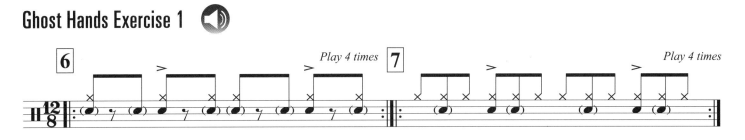

Ghost Hands Exercise 2

The bass drum is added starting at Example 9B and Example 10 is a paradiddle groove.

LESSON 8: JAZZ COMPING

In jazz drumming, "comping" is one of the most essential elements. "Comping" comes from the word "compliment" or "accompany." So the drummer is trying to compliment and accompany the ride cymbal and the music. This will provide interest to the groove, add variety to the time, and foster communication with the other musicians.

Comping Exercise

Let's play a steady ride cymbal and hi-hat pattern while introducing some snare and bass drum comp figures. Please keep in mind that all rhythmic figures are played in a triplet feel, or swing feel.

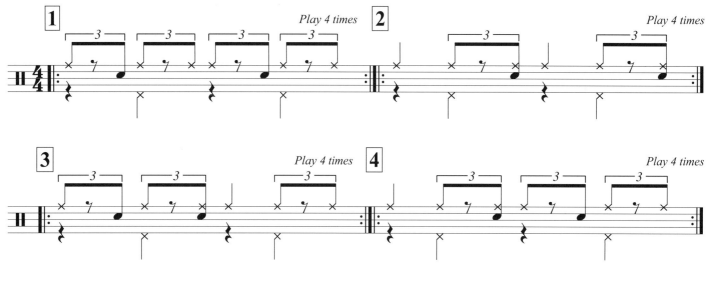

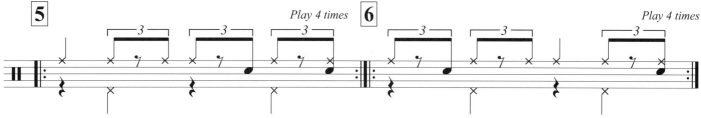

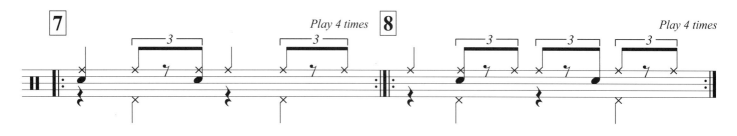

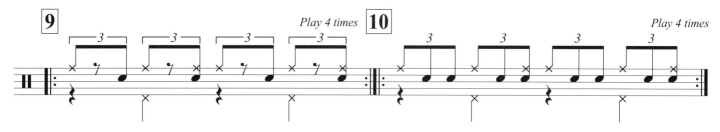

Below are the four basic jazz **articulations**, representing the degree to which notes are separated or connected:

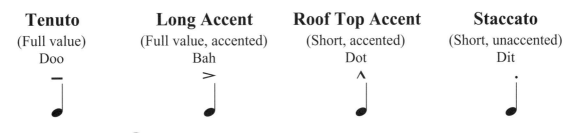

Tenuto	**Long Accent**	**Roof Top Accent**	**Staccato**
(Full value)	(Full value, accented)	(Short, accented)	(Short, unaccented)
Doo	Bah	Dot	Dit

Isolated Comp Rhythms 🔊

Now let's try playing the isolated comp figures. Visualize the ride cymbal and hi-hat pattern in your head while playing the written rhythms. Remember to swing all 8th notes. Here are some of the most commonly used:

🔊 ▶️ **"THANKS FOR THE COMPLIMENT"**

While continuing the jazz ride pattern with beats 2 and 4 on the hi-hat, play each variation below four times and proceed. Feel free to mix up the snare and bass drum, as heard on the audio demonstration track.

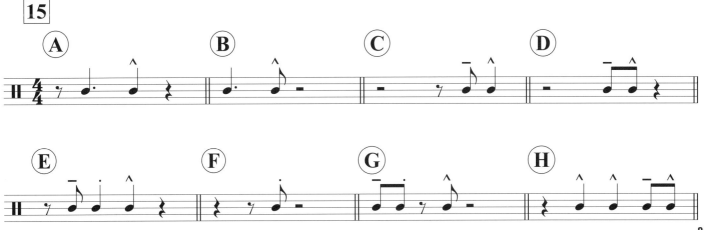

LESSON 9: JAZZ STICKINGS

> **QUICK TIP** – Practicing accents within a triplet jazz base is very helpful for creating new fill ideas.

The rhythmic flow of jazz drumming is centered on the triplet-based 8th note. The drummer must start with a single surface, such as the snare drum, before moving around the drumset. Creating a fluid motion of legato strokes will be helpful when playing fills, set-ups, and solos (you'll learn more about set-ups and solos in the coming lessons).

Jazz Sticking Exercise

Two sticking methods should be used for the following exercises:

1. Hand to Hand: R L R L R L

2. Right-Hand Lead: the right hand plays all of the accents and the left hand fills in between.

Add soft, "feathered" bass drum quarter notes with the right foot and hi-hat on 2 and 4 with the left foot, and play with a swing feel. After you're comfortable playing the exercises on the snare, change up the accents by playing them on different drums, as heard on the audio demonstration track.

22

Now try to play a continuous flow of 8th-note triplets around the drumset using different surfaces and sticking patterns. The goal here is to develop a smooth flow using triplets around the drums.

Smooth Triplet Exercise

Focus on playing smooth, continuous triplets around the drums.

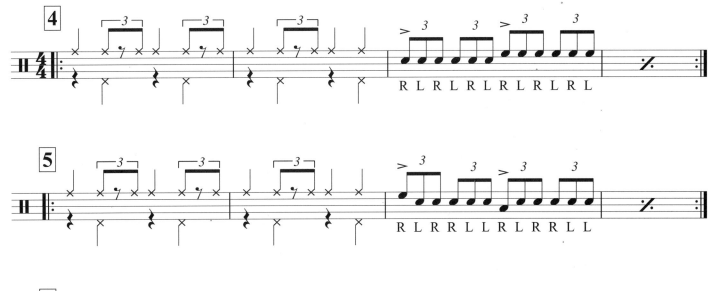

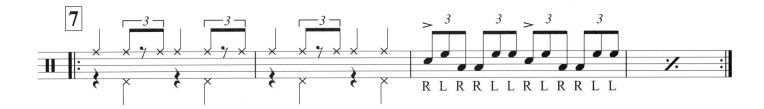

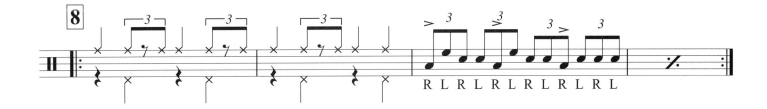

LESSON 10: CHART INTERPRETATION

UNDERSTANDING CHART NOTATION

Quite often when a drummer reads a chart, the majority of what he or she plays is not on the printed music. The drummer has a unique responsibility to decide what to play from the information given on the chart. This is referred to as **interpretation**.

The main role of the drummer is to provide solid time and establish an appropriate groove (or feel) for the music. The drummer may also play some of the ensemble or section figures that are usually written above the staff, or on the staff (sometimes with larger notes called slash notation). Composers differ on how they notate these figures. Here are three different examples of what the same drum chart might look like:

Written Above the Staff:

Written on the Staff (in Slash Notation):

Written as Drum Notation:

But, what happens during rests? When reading a drumset chart, a rest means one of two things:

1. Actually rest and do *not* play, or

2. Insert a fill

Most often the word "fill" is not found in music, and the drummer must use his or her intuition to decide when one should be played. Main accents are often notated and fills can be used tastefully in a rest. Longer fill sections are usually marked in the music and some may just say "solo."

How to interpret figures and rests? This is not a simple answer, but there are definitely some guidelines that will be discussed in the following lessons. Sometimes it is best to just play some simple reinforced rhythms on the snare drum. And then, after you get more comfortable, use different drums and cymbals to add color.

Drum Chart:

Simple Reinforcement:

Add Other Drums for More Variation:

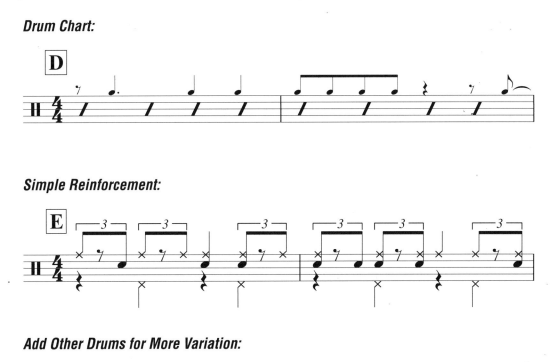

Following are several two-measure examples to practice. Each is jazz-based and played with a swing feel.

Chart Example 1
(cont.)

Chart Example 2
(cont.)

Chart Example 3
(cont.)

LESSON 11: SET-UPS

> **QUICK TIP –** Some of the most notable jazz big band leaders include Chick Webb, Duke Ellington, Gene Krupa, Benny Goodman, Count Basie, and Buddy Rich.

SHORT AND LONG NOTES

In big band music, the drummer should know how to properly play short notes and long notes. **Short notes** are commonly played with the snare drum (or bass drum, or even choked hi-hat cymbal) against the standard ride pattern. Short notes can occur on both downbeats and upbeats, but rarely require a set-up.

Short-Note Figures

Here are a few variations with short-note figures:

Long notes are usually tied, creating a value greater than a quarter note. They are played on a cymbal and bass drum (or snare drum) at the same time. Long notes usually have a **set-up** into the figure. In other words, you are playing a small fill that leads into an ensemble entrance that you literally "kick." Let's try a few exercises using the snare drum to "set up," and then the bass drum and crash to "kick" the ensemble figure.

Long-Note Figures

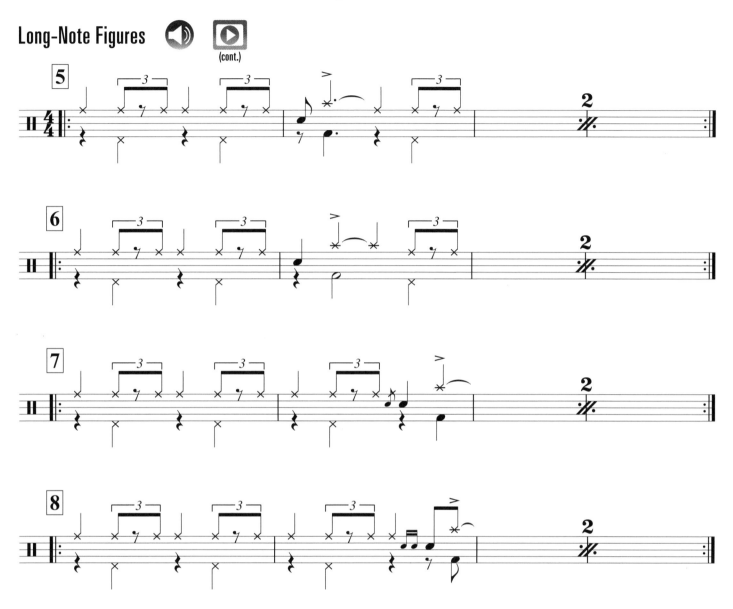

Most commonly played set-up figures include the quarter note (lines 5–6), flam (line 7), and ruff (line 8). A **ruff** is like a flam but played with more than one grace note. The stick is allowed to bounce for the grace notes.

Several things can determine the kind of fill or set-up that should be played.

Slow Tempo Set-Up

16th notes work well for slow-tempo fills and set-ups.

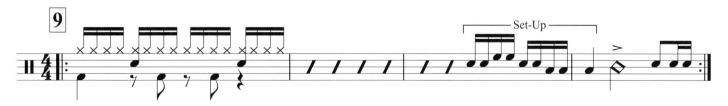

Medium Tempo Set-Up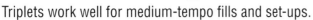

Triplets work well for medium-tempo fills and set-ups.

Up-Tempo Set-Up

Simple, one-count, downbeat fills and set-ups work well for **up-tempo** music (fast tempos).

"GO GET IT"

LESSON 12: LONG VS. SHORT SOUNDS

> **QUICK TIP –** In jazz-style music, quarter notes are usually played staccato, while 8th notes are usually played legato.

Another important aspect of chart reading is the ability of the drummer to match the note lengths of the ensemble with those of the drumset. Learning to match these articulations (note shape) means the drummer has to think like a horn player.

Also refer to Lesson 8 for additional information on articulations.

Short Articulations (Might use snare drum, rimshot, hi-hat choke):
 Staccato (·)
 Marcato (housetop, ^)
 Short Note Value

Long Articulations (Might use cymbal crashes):
 Tenuto (−)
 Tie (⌒)
 Long Note Value

Ensemble Exercise 1

Let's try a few examples of kicking isolated figures with various articulations. You should be able to "sing" these lines as well as play them. Check out Lesson 8 to review the syllables used to count and verbalize jazz articulations.

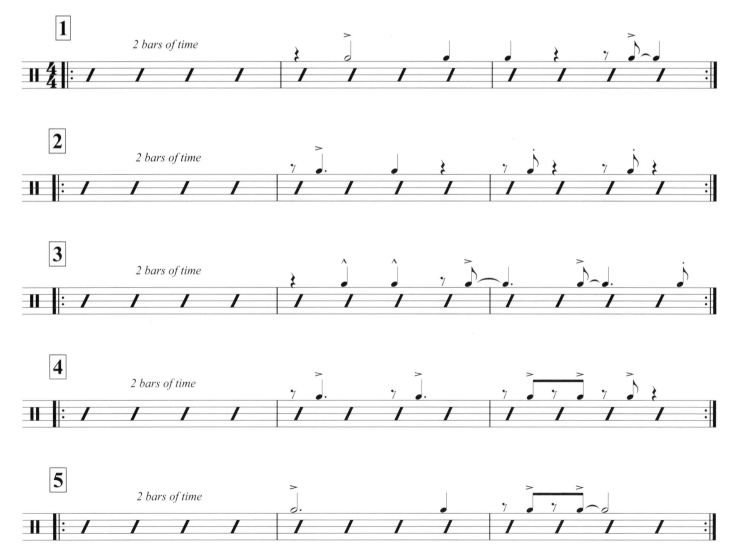

Ensemble Exercise 2

"The 8th-Note Rule" is a general guideline for deciding what notes to play when there is more than just a single 8th note by itself. When an 8th note is standing by itself (as in lines 1–5) with nothing after it, it will usually be played as an accent. If the 8th note is followed by another note (or more), it becomes a "filler" note before the accent (see lines 6–9). An exception to this rule would occur when there are four 8th notes together. In this case, you would accent the first and last notes (see lines 10 and 11).

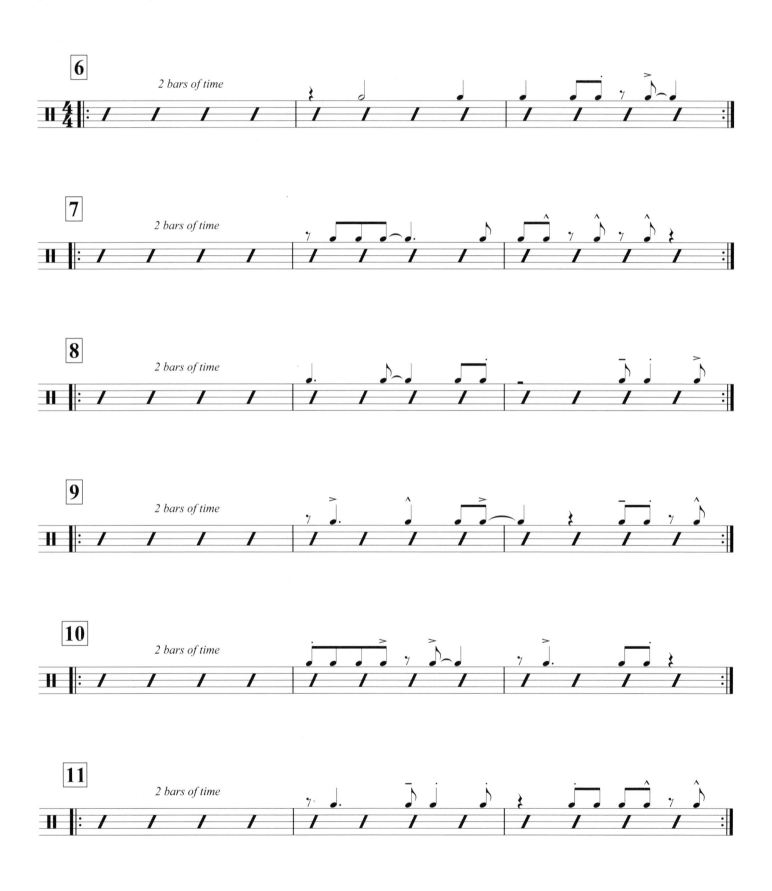

"SWINGIN' JOE"

In the following song, you'll see a new routing direction: ***D.C. al Fine***. "D.C." stands for the Italian phrase "da capo," meaning "from the beginning." This direction tells you to return to the beginning of the song and play up to the word "Fine," which means "end."

LESSON 13: DRUM SOLOING

The two words "drum solo" can bring fear to drummers with limited experience. A drum solo can range in length from one bar to eight bars or longer. Sometimes a drum solo is used to help transition into another section, or even to help change the mood from the current groove. Every drummer should have a library of simple one-bar phrases like these:

One-Bar Solo Phrases

Play all the lines with a swing feel, except for line 8.

Creating a Drum Solo

Here are some tips for creating drum solos in a jazz style with a swing feel. **Note:** on the accompanying audio, the following examples are played in continuous succession across one track.

Repetition

Repetition means taking a musical phrase or section of music and repeating exactly the same phrase or altering the idea. Play four bars of time and then solo for four bars. This is commonly known as "trading fours."

Orchestration

Experiment using different drums, cymbals, rimshots, etc.

Dynamics

Using different levels of dynamics will give your solo energy and even more personality.

Add Rests

A really easy way to add variety to your solo is to insert some space by using rests.

Add Rests Within the Phrase

Embellishments

Embellish means to "decorate" the music. This can be achieved by using accents, flams, ruffs, rimshots, etc.

 "LUCKY SEVEN"

The final exercise is a short tune with some solo breaks. Take note that there will be no click on the audio tracks during the solo. Therefore, you must keep a steady pulse and re-enter in time.

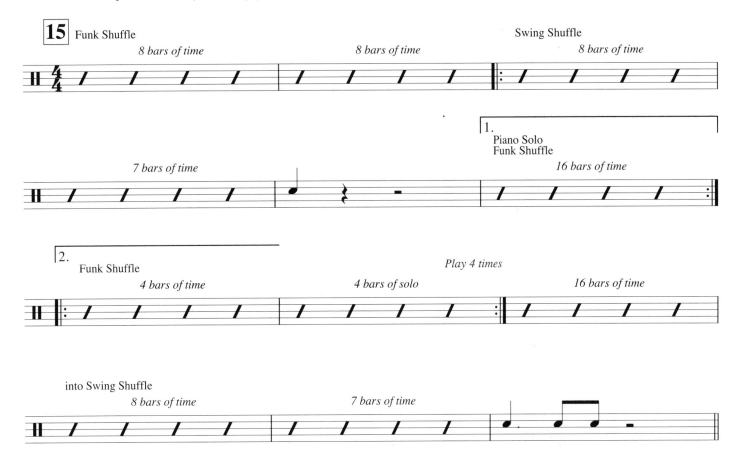

LESSON 14: JAZZ CHARTS

> **QUICK TIP** – A drummer uses the trial and error method when sight reading a piece of music.
> It is better to "underplay" than "overplay" the first time through.

Following are two sample jazz charts containing many of the concepts you have learned thus far.

"JAZZ CHART 1"

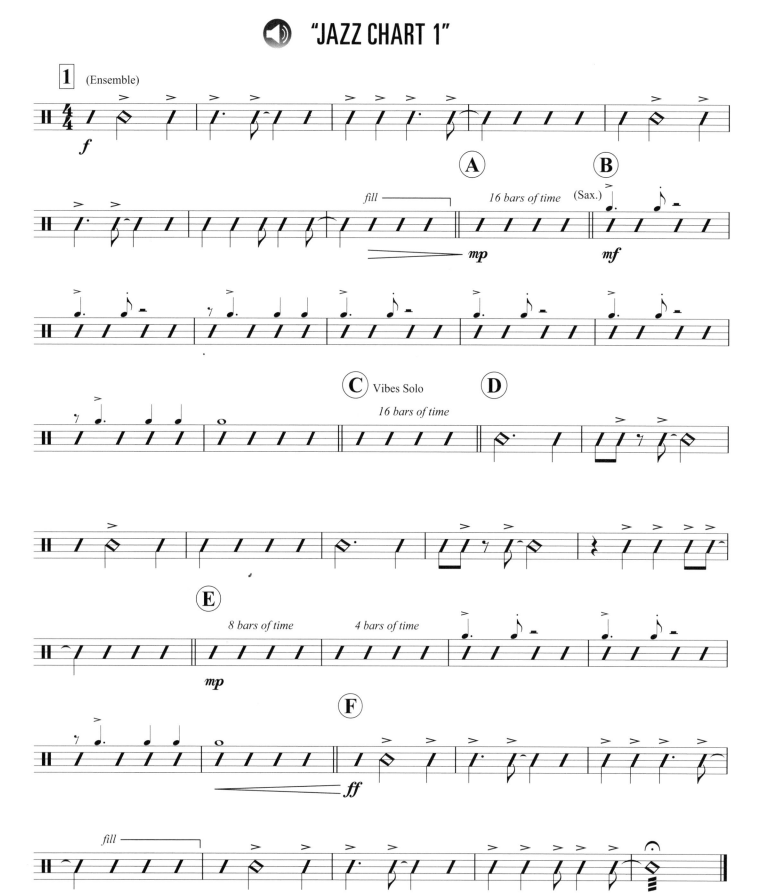

LESSON 15: ROCK/FUNK CHARTS

QUICK TIP – Less is sometimes more! Simple grooves and simple fills can often be more appropriate than busy playing. Use your ears to make smart musical choices.

ROCK/FUNK CHART READING

When playing a chart in the style of rock or funk, there are a few things to remember:

1. Use any written idea or reference of the desired groove to help determine what you might play.

2. Listen to the bass player and rhythm section for style and rhythmic ostinato.

3. Funk fills usually set up the downbeat of the next measure, but sometimes a funk fill can end on a syncopated figure as seen below:

Funk Fill 1

Funk Fill 2

4. The drummer does not have to play *everything* they see on a chart. But they must identify the different roles he or she will play throughout the music. What is the primary groove? Does the groove change? Are there any soloists? What figures should I catch? When/if should I go to hi-hat vs. ride cymbal?

Funk Chart Exercise

As you look at example 4, some choices have to be made about how you are going to catch the figures starting in measure 5. Many of these figures can picked up within the groove. In other words, keep the backbeat on 2 and 4 as much as possible while playing some of the cues with bass drum, hi-hat, or other parts of the kit. Using the snare drum to kick many of the rhythms will prevent the groove from flowing evenly.

"ROCK CHART 1"

LESSON 16: BRUSH PLAYING

Playing with brushes is another skill often used by jazz drummers. This distinct sound can commonly be heard in standard tempo songs, but especially in slow tempo ballads. Brushes can provide a warm, smooth, and fluid mood at lower volumes and at all tempos. Unlike playing with sticks, brush playing requires a type of sustained (constant) motion.

Brush Pattern 1

This basic brush pattern can be used at most tempos. The left hand will circle clockwise in half notes starting around the 10 o'clock position on beats 1 and 3. Arrive at 4 to 5 o'clock on beats 2 and 4. Try to keep the left hand smooth and legato. The right hand will play the jazz ride pattern by gently tapping on the drumhead from the right (on beats 1 and 3) to the left (on beats 2 and 4). The hands will actually cross on beats 2 and 4, but keep the left-hand sound smooth and consistent.

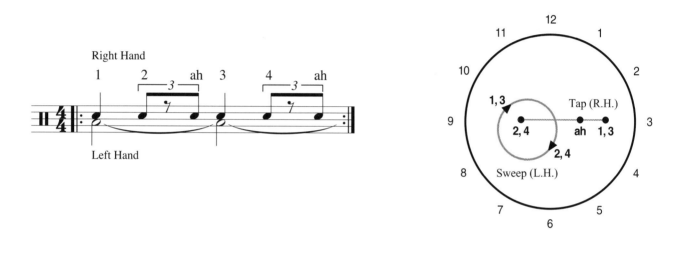

"MISS JONES"

This next tune is a medium swing played with brushes. You'll see a new marking in the last few measures of this chart: "rit." This stands for **ritardando** and means to gradually slow down.

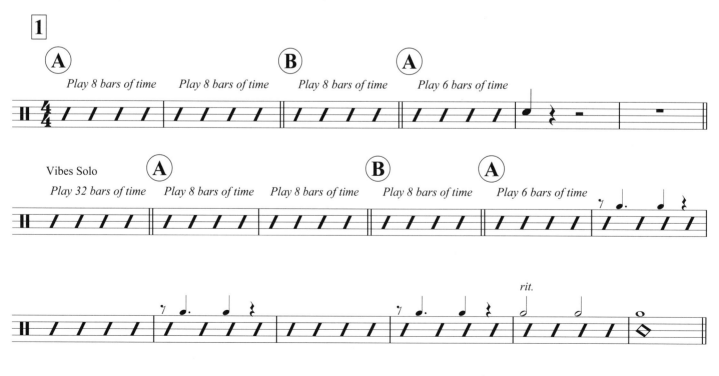

Brush Pattern 2

This ballad pattern can be used for very slow tempos. Practice each hand separately starting at the 12 o'clock position and brush a circle in quarter notes. The left hand moves clockwise while the right hand brushes counterclockwise. Try a slight push of the brush into the head on each downbeat to help establish some weight for the quarter-note pulse. When you have achieved a consistent legato motion, put the hands together. Each hand circles in quarter notes while coming towards the other on the downbeats.

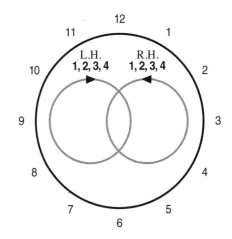

Brush Pattern 2 Variation

This works well for a swing ballad tempo. The left hand circles quarter notes while the right hand plays the jazz ride pattern.

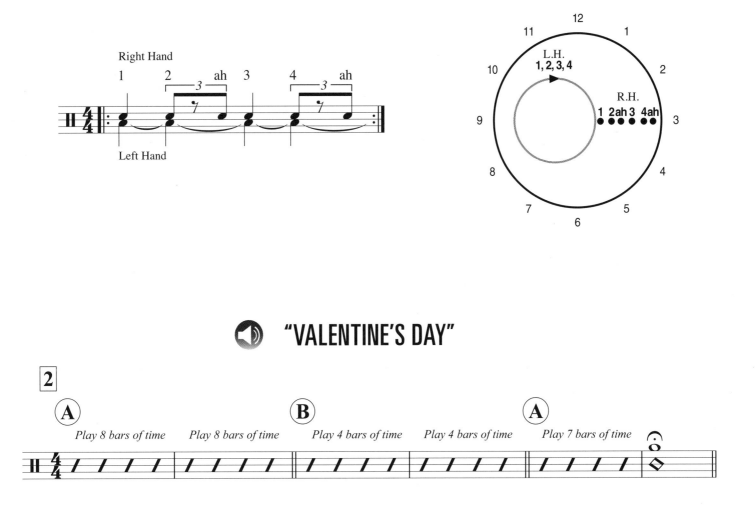

"VALENTINE'S DAY"

LESSON 17: COUNTRY DRUMMING

> **QUICK TIP –** The "Nashville Number System" is a common system used by Nashville musicians when reading and writing chord charts. Each chord change in a tune has a corresponding number.

COUNTRY VARIATIONS ▶️

Country is a type of American music that developed in the southern part of the United States in the late 1800s. Originating with Western swing, "honky tonk" style, the Grand Ole Opry, country shuffle, country pop, the "outlaw movement," Opryland, country rock, the "Nashville sound," and exploding into modern country.

Modern country most often uses a shuffle (or straight 8th-note) groove.

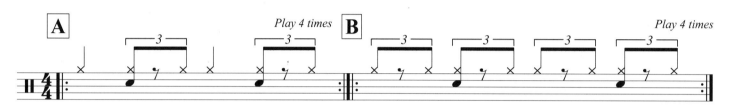

Country Shuffle 🔊

Here is a shuffle using a brush with the right hand on the snare and cross-stick (also called **side-stick** or **rim knock**) with the left hand on beats 2 and 4:

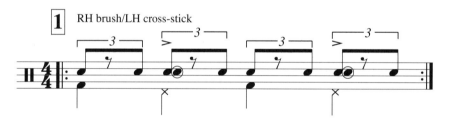

Traditional Shuffle 🔊

Here is a more traditional country shuffle, followed by the same beat with a half-time feel.

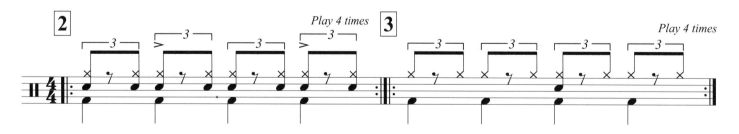

Country rock and pop includes more straight 8th-note beats and features many snare and bass drum patterns similar to those found in rock and funk music. However, a country groove may have a creative approach to an old idea.

Country Rock/Pop 🔊

Playing a contrasting sound on beat 4 can add some texture and/or energy to a country pattern, as seen in these next two examples.

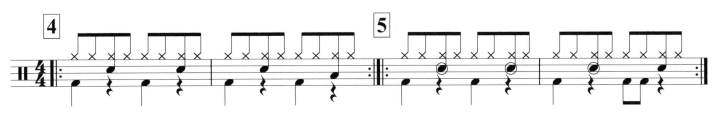

Snare Drum Pattern 1 🔊

Play the right hand hi-hat pattern on the snare drum.

Snare Drum Pattern 2 🔊

Now try 16ths on the snare drum.

🔊 **"BIG TEX"**

LESSON 18: HIP-HOP/DANCE BEATS

> **QUICK TIP** – The common trademark of hip-hop music is the swing feel. However, most half-time feels in hip-hop style are usually played straight rather than swung.

Hip-hop began in New York City in the late 1970s and became extremely popular in the 1990s. In this style, all of the 16th notes should have a slight swing. As a result of the mixture of rock and funk grooves, the possible variations are almost endless.

Hip-Hop Grooves

Remember to slightly swing the 16th notes.

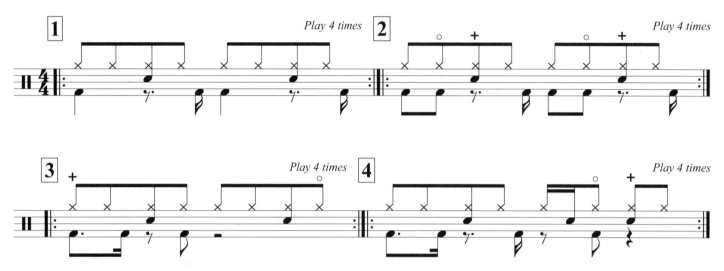

Also play the above variations with alternated, shuffled 16th notes on the hi-hat.

"GET READY"
(cont.)

Another type of groove that spawned from a combination of hip-hop and disco music was house dance music. All of these beats were played around the tempo of 120 bpm, similar to disco. Use of the open hi-hat and "four on the floor" is also a big characteristic of house.

House Grooves

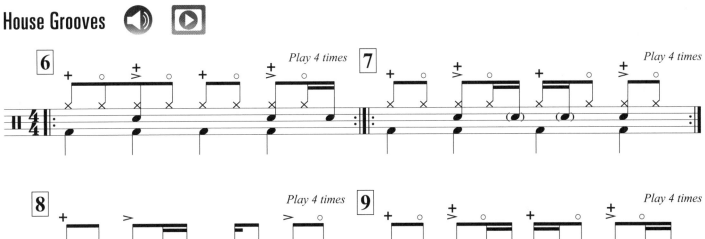

"HOUSE MONEY"

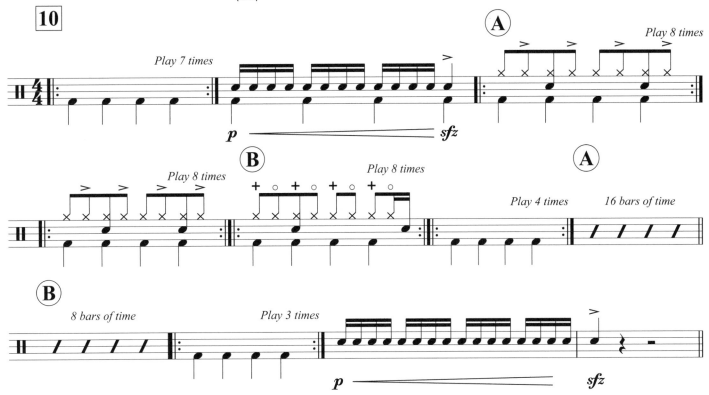

LESSON 19: CALYPSO/SOCA

> **QUICK TIP –** "Day-O (The Banana Boat Song)" is a classic calypso recording made
> by Harry Belafonte and based on a traditional Jamaican folk song.

Caribbean music is a combination of many different musical cultures. The rhythms and instruments (like steel drum) are often referred to as "island music." Two of the most commonly played styles within this genre include **calypso** and **soca**. The calypso beat usually has a bit more syncopation in the bass drum pattern. Here are a few variations:

Calypso Variations

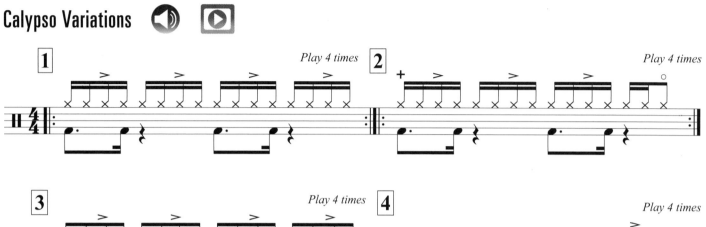

"CARIBBEAN CRUISE"

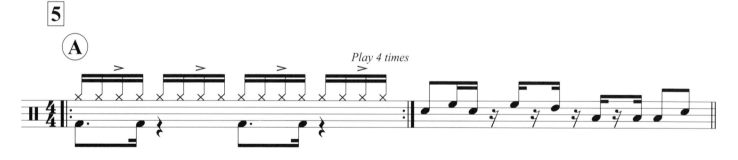

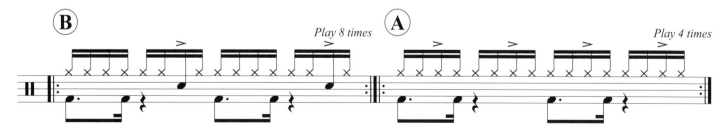

In the 1970s, disco was the soul of American music. The mixture of disco and calypso melded into soca. This style features a high-energy groove that gets its pulse from driving quarter notes on the bass drum with the hi-hat opening on each upbeat.

Soca Grooves

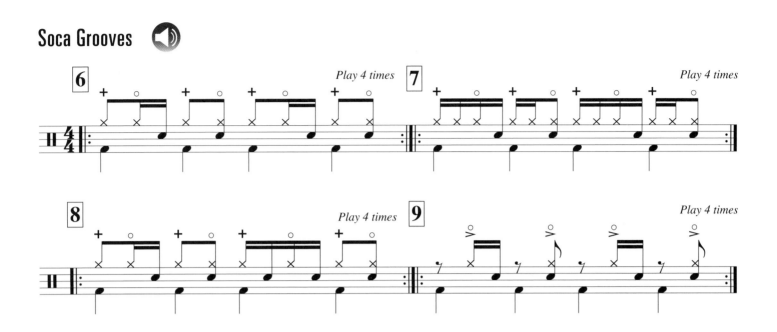

"SOCA SPIRIT"

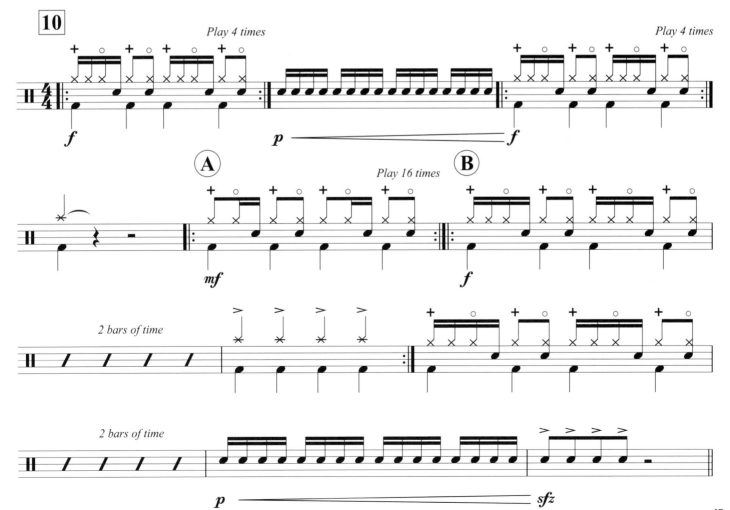

LESSON 20: AFRO-CUBAN STYLES

QUICK TIP – One of the most recognized cha-cha grooves in Latin and American pop music is entitled "Oye Como Va"—written by Tito Puente and famously redone by Santana.

The term **Afro-Cuban** refers to the blending of music from Africa, Cuba, Puerto Rico, and the Dominican Republic. The merging of all these cultures resulted in many new forms of music. Some of these will be discussed in the next few lessons.

CLAVE

The pulse of Afro-Cuban music is the **clave**, which means "key" in Spanish. The clave is both an instrument and a rhythm. As the cymbal ride pattern is to jazz, the clave is to Afro-Cuban music. There are two measures in a clave pattern. One measure has two notes and the other has three notes. Claves are two pieces of wood that are struck together. This rhythm can also be played on almost any part of the drumset.

2:3 Clave Patterns

The following exercises feature the 2:3 clave rhythm, with two notes in the first measure and three in the second. A **rhumba** is a popular Cuban dance where the clave includes a slight displacement of the third note (beat 4) in the second measure. Each clave below is played alone first and then along with 8th notes on the hi-hat.

2:3 Son Clave

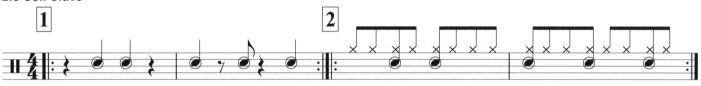

2:3 Rhumba Clave

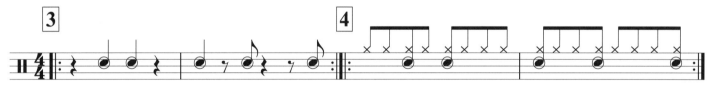

3:2 Clave Patterns
(cont.)

Next up is the 3:2 clave rhythm, with three notes in the first measure and two in the second. Each clave is played alone first and then along with 8th notes on the hi-hat.

3:2 Son Clave

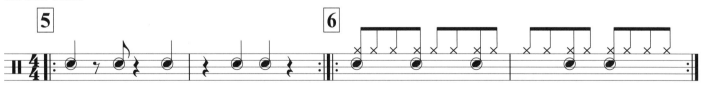

3:2 Rhumba Clave

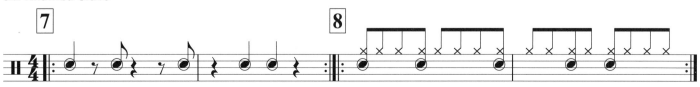

TUMBAO

Tumbao is a repeated rhythm that is usually played by the bass player and/or conga player in Afro-Cuban music. The drumset player can reinforce this with the bass drum.

Tumbao Patterns

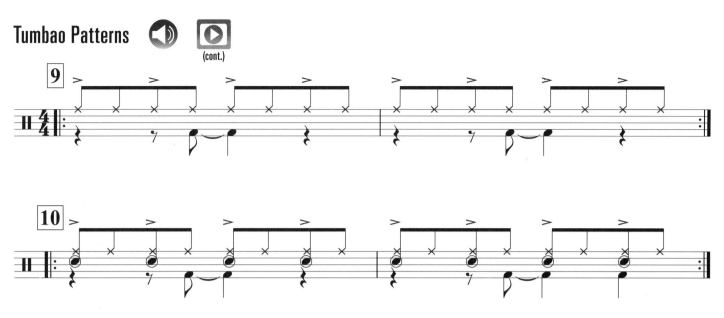

CASCARA

Another important Afro-Cuban rhythm is called the **cascara**. When used on the drumset, this rhythm can be played with the right hand on the closed hi-hat, ride cymbal, rim or shell of floor tom, cowbell, or the cymbal bell.

Cascara Patterns

Here is the basic cascara rhythm, also shown with clave and tumbao.

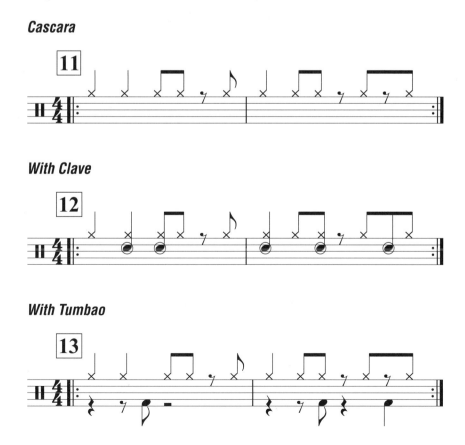

CHA-CHA

The **cha-cha** comes from the cha-cha-cha, an Afro-Cuban salsa dance. It is very similar to a mambo but played at a slower tempo. (The mambo is covered in the following lesson.) The cha-cha groove starts with a quarter-note cowbell rhythm and 8th notes played by the guiro (or on the hi-hat). In the following variations, the cowbell part can be played on the ride cymbal bell (line 14) or with the cross-stick technique (line 15–16).

Cha-Cha Patterns

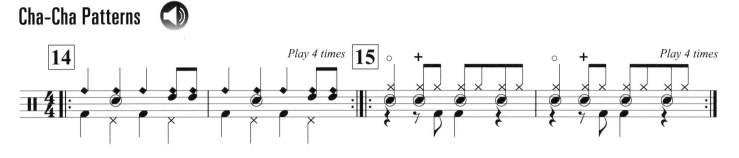

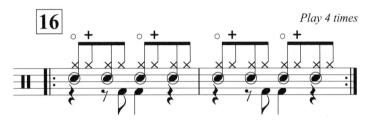

"LA BAHAMA"

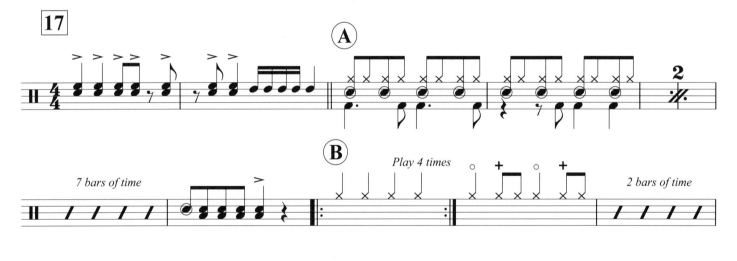

LESSON 21: MORE AFRO-CUBAN STYLES

QUICK TIP – The groove of Afro-Cuban music comes from the slight swing feel that is characteristic in this style. It can sometimes be in between 8th notes and triplets. Listening to music of this style will help you learn to capture the authentic feel.

MAMBO

The **mambo** may be the most popular of all of the Afro-Cuban musical styles. Most often a mambo is performed with several percussionists, so a drumset player has a challenge to cover these parts with only four limbs. The right hand usually covers the mambo bell pattern, the left hand covers the conga pattern, the bass drum plays the tumbao pattern (or variation), and the hi-hat can play on beats 1 and 3, or 2 and 4. The mambo is a two-measure pattern that is based on the son clave, starting with the two or three pattern.

Traditional Mambo

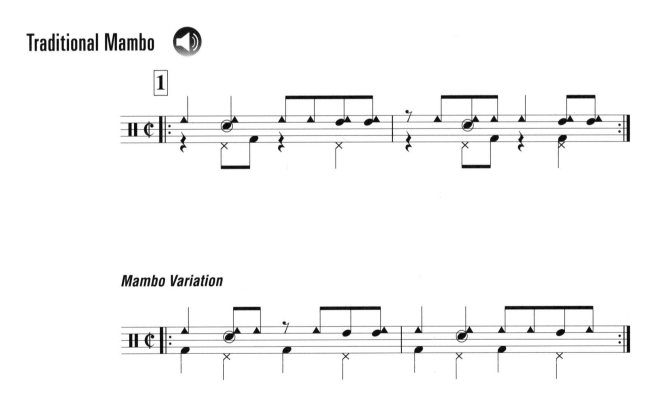

Mambo Variation

The term **salsa** refers to a form or style of Afro-Cuban music that was actually created in the United States in the 1970s. Like the mambo, the primary instruments are congas, timbales, bongos, claves, and cowbells. Here is the basic salsa form:

Intro – Verse – Montuno *(starts with piano solo)* **– Mambo – Verse – Outro**

🔊 "PASS THE PICANTE"

SONGO

Unlike any of the previously mentioned Afro-Cuban grooves, the **songo** was actually conceived with the drumset rhythm first and then additional percussion instruments were added. Songo rhythms are built from a mixture of various Afro-Cuban musical styles. The right hand usually plays a steady pulse, the bass drum plays the tumbao rhythm, and the snare fills in with syncopated notes (some ghosted as well).

Songo Patterns

Standard Songo Groove

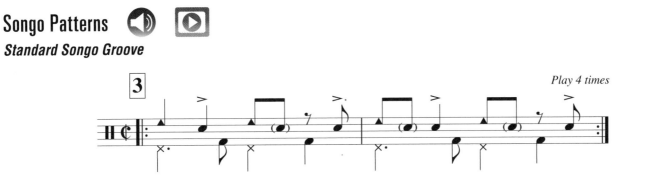

Songo Groove Variations

"CUBAN DANCE"

In the following song, you'll see a new routing direction: **D.S. al Fine**. "D.S." stands for the Italian phrase "dal segno," meaning "from the sign." This direction tells you to return to the sign (𝄋) and play up to the "Fine."

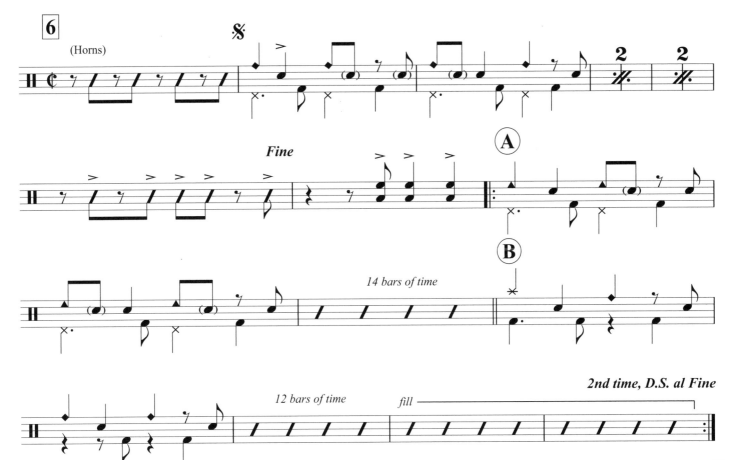

LESSON 22: BRAZILIAN STYLES

BOSSA NOVA

Bossa nova may be the most popular Latin groove originating from Brazil. It is much more subtle and laid back compared to other types of Latin grooves. A lighter approach and touch is recommended for this style. It should be played in a smooth and seamless manner.

Bossa Nova Patterns

Usually, a medium-tempo bossa nova is played with cross-stick. There are many variations of the cross-stick pattern that can be played. The bass drum has a repeated rhythm throughout. First, try playing 8th notes on the hi-hat with the right hand along with the repeated bass drum rhythm, and then add the cross-stick patterns as shown in the following examples:

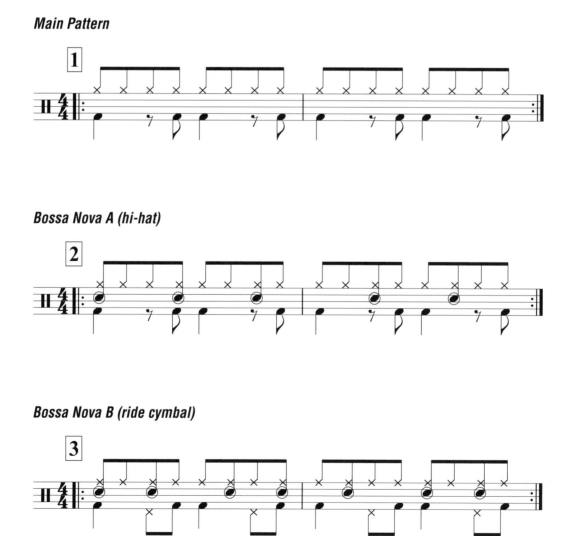

Main Pattern

Bossa Nova A (hi-hat)

Bossa Nova B (ride cymbal)

🔊 "BIG BOSS OF NOVA"

In the following song, you'll see a new routing direction: **_D.S. al Coda_**. As you learned earlier, "D.S." tells you to return to the sign (𝄋) in the chart. Next, "al Coda" directs you to play up to the "To Coda" sign (⊕). When you reach it, you should go directly to where the other similar coda sign is located and play to the end of the piece.

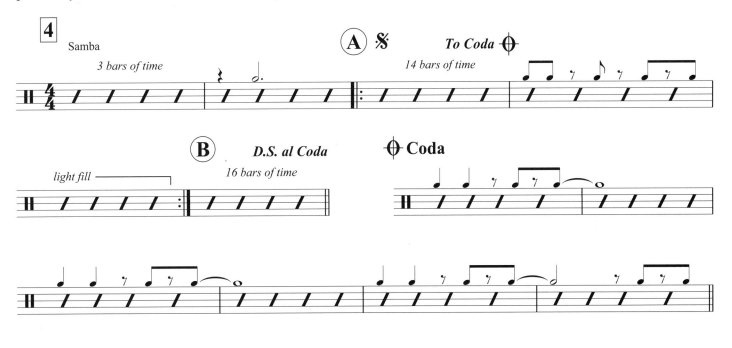

SAMBA ▶️

Samba is another popular rhythm from Brazil. This musical style comes from the many samba bands that perform at the Carnaval Festival each year in Rio. These bands are filled with many musicians that contribute to the exciting and hypnotic grooves that fill the air. The percussion instruments found in the samba band include the surdo, the caixa, the repenique, the tamborim, and the ganza (shaker). Each of these instruments play a specific rhythm which all blend together for an incredible energy and excitement. Since there are so many instruments and rhythms going on, a drumset player has some freedom and creativity to choose which ones to play on the set to create this type of groove.

Similar to the bossa nova, the bass drum also has a repeated pattern throughout. Here is the foot pattern:

Samba Patterns 🔊

Slow to Medium Samba

Jazz Samba

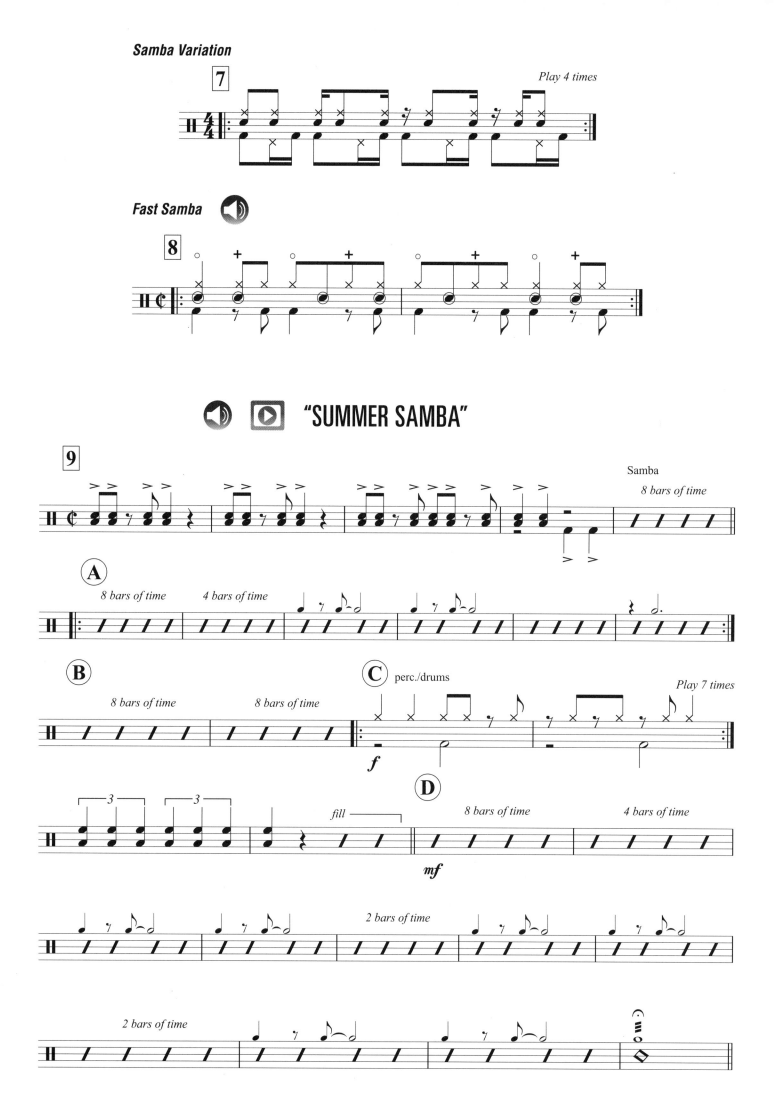

Samba Variation

7 Play 4 times

Fast Samba

8

"SUMMER SAMBA"

9 Samba
8 bars of time

Ⓐ
8 bars of time   4 bars of time

Ⓑ   Ⓒ perc./drums   Play 7 times
8 bars of time   8 bars of time

Ⓓ
fill   8 bars of time   4 bars of time

2 bars of time

2 bars of time

ENCORE #3

Congratulations for making it through Book 2 of the *Hal Leonard Drumset Method!* Here are two full song charts for study and practice. Remember to download the extra content that comes with this book. It includes lots of bonus practice material—accent exercises, syncopation studies, comping exercises, ostinato patterns, and more!

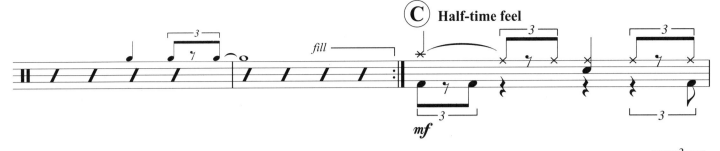

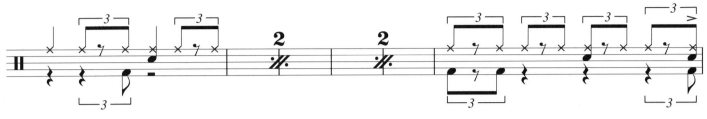

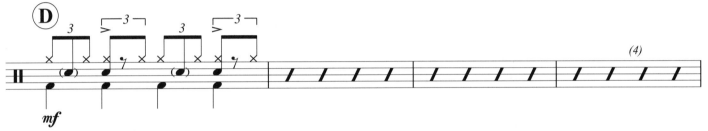

ENCORE #4

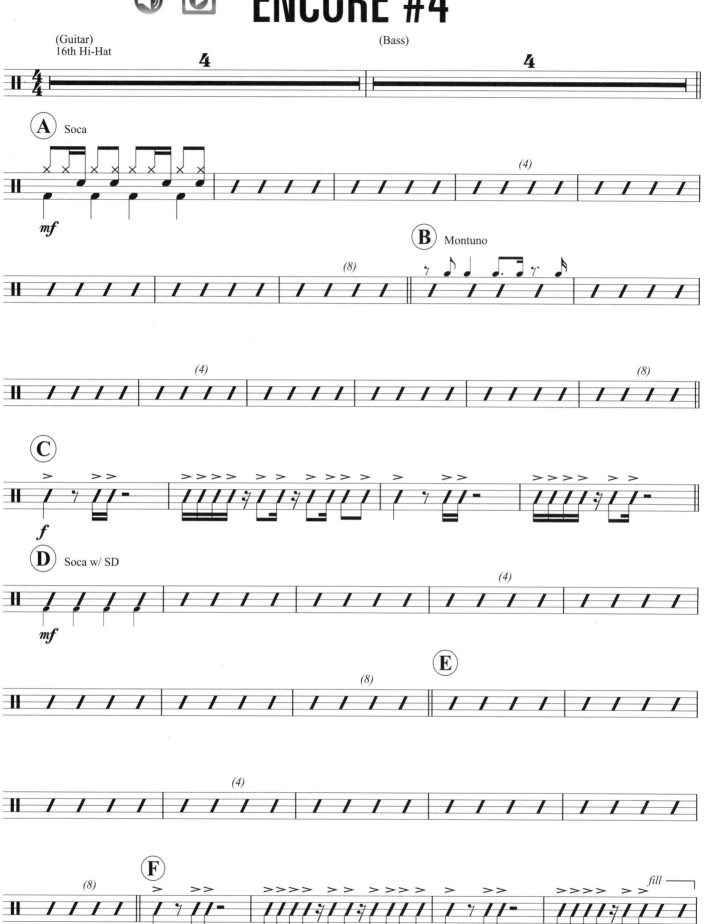

Songo Groove

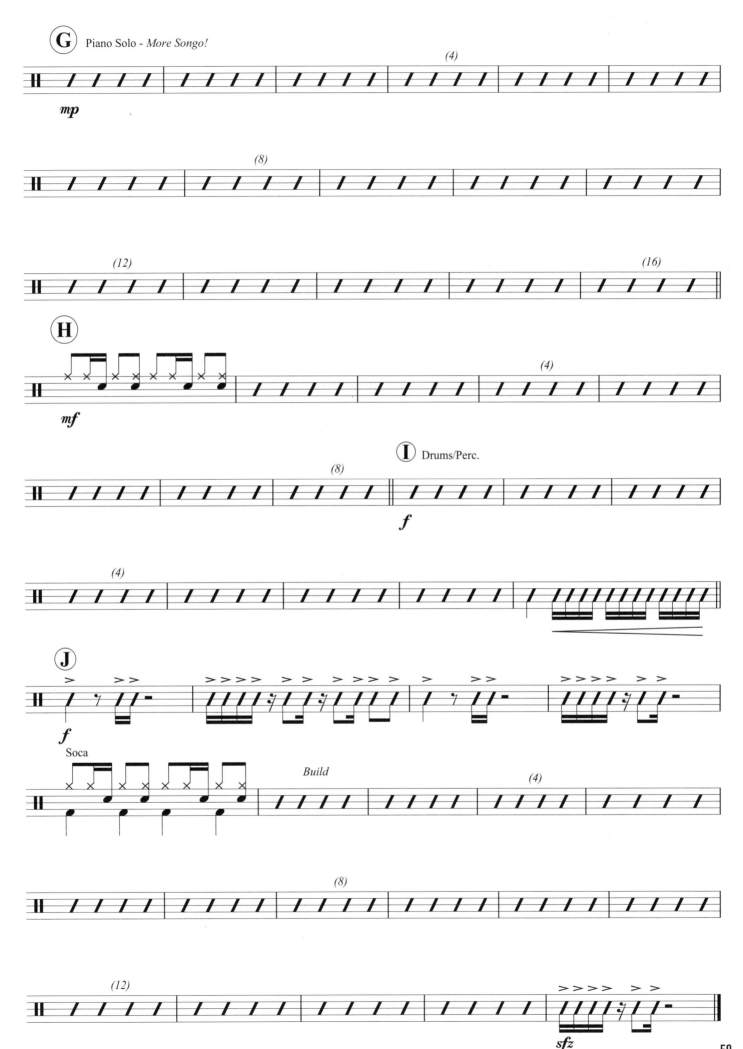

GLOSSARY

A

Accelerando – (*accel.*) Gradually faster, accelerating.

Afro-Cuban – The blending of music styles from Africa, Cuba, Puerto Rico, and the Dominican Republic.

Articulation – The degree to which notes are separated or connected, such as staccato or legato.

B

Bell – Also called the dome or cup. The raised section of a cymbal immediately surrounding the hole.

Bossa Nova – Popular dance from Brazil.

C

Cascara – Afro-Cuban rhythm that is most often played on the shell of a drum.

Calypso – Style of Afro-Caribbean music that originated in Trinidad and Tobago.

Cha-Cha – Afro-Cuban groove that came from a salsa dance known as the cha-cha-cha.

Clave – *Key*: two-measure rhythm that serves as a reference point for all rhythms and melodies found in Cuban music.

Coda Sign $\oplus$ – Used to end a musical composition. The sign tells you to jump forward to the end section, called a coda.

Comping – Refers to playing "comp"-limentary rhythms with various limbs, usually in the jazz style.

Cross-Stick – Also called side-stick or rim knock. Played by laying stick across drumhead and clicking shaft of stick on the rim.

D

D.C. – *Da Capo*: repeat to the beginning.

D.S. – *Dal Segno*: repeat to the D.S. sign ⅜.

Dome – Also called the bell or cup. The raised section of a cymbal immediately surrounding the hole.

E

Embellishment – Decorating a musical idea by using accents, dynamics, articulations, etc.

F

Fermata ⌢ – Symbol indicating to hold a tone or rest beyond the written value, at the discretion of the performer(s).

Fill – Used to "fill-in" space, usually occurring at phrase endings.

Fine – End

Funk – Music genre that originated in the 1960s when African-American musicians created a rhythmic, danceable type of music that mixed jazz, soul, and R&B music.

G

Ghost Note – Note that is played lightly under the main notes, most often on the snare drum, and typically notated with parentheses.

H

Half-Time Feel – This occurs when the backbeat shifts from 2 and 4 to beat 3, creating a new feel.

Hip-Hop – Musical style that started in the 1970s in New York City and became popular world-wide in the 1990s. Some distinct elements include rap, breakdancing, and graffiti art.

House – Type of dance music that grew from the combination of hip-hop and disco.

I

Interpretation – Refers to the drummer's ability of deciding what to play and how when reading a musical chart.

Island Music – Refers to music found in the Caribbean region, usually including steel drums.

L

Long Note – Type of chart notation that calls for a full-value note articulation, commonly played with a cymbal and bass drum (or snare drum) at the same time.

M

Mambo – Recognized as the most popular of all the Afro-Cuban musical styles.

Marcato – ^ *Marked*: short, accented articulation with a "housetop" marking above note.

O

Ostinato – Musical figure that is repetitive.

R

Rhumba – Popular Cuban dance with a distinct syncopated clave pattern.

Rim Knock – Also called cross-stick and side-stick. Played by laying stick across drumhead and clicking shaft of stick on the rim.

Rimshot – Played by striking the drumhead and rim at the same time.

Ritardando – (*rit.*) *Delaying*, becoming gradually slower.

Ruff – Drum rudiment similar to a flam but played with more than one grace note. The stick is allowed to bounce for the grace notes.

S

Salsa – Refers to a form/style of Afro-Cuban music created in the United States in the 1970s. Form usually includes a montuno section with a unique bell pattern.

Samba – The most famous Brazilian musical form. Developed in Bahia and Rio de Janiero during early part of 20th century.

Set-Up – Small fill that leads into an ensemble figure.

Short Note – Type of chart notation that calls for a short articulation, commonly played with the snare drum (or bass drum, or even choked hi-hat cymbal) against a standard ride pattern.

Shuffle – A rhythm based off the first and third note of each triplet.

Side-Stick – Also called cross-stick and rim knock. Played by laying stick across drumhead and clicking shaft of stick on the rim.

Slash Notation – Slash symbols instead of notes on a staff that indicate "time-keeping" in drum parts. Usually means to continue what was previously played for a specified number of beats.

Soca – A high-energy style of music that came from Amercian disco and calypso.

Songo – The only Afro-Cuban groove that was conceived on the drumset, as opposed to percussion instruments.

Staccato – · *Detached*: Short, unaccented articulation.

Syncopation – The placement of rhythmic accents on upbeats or weak beats.

T

Tenuto – ⁻ *Held*: Full value articulation

Trading Fours – Playing four bars of time and then a solo for four bars.

Tumbao – Repeated rhythm played by the conga player in Afro-Cuban music.

U

Up-Tempo – Fast

LISTENING REFERENCES

The listening references below represent some basic examples of the musical styles learned in this book. Each is listed in chronological order so you can trace the development of each style. Please remember this is only a very small sampling and there are so many more you can find. Listen to as much music as you can!

ROCK
Early Rock
Elvis Presley
Chuck Berry
Little Richard

Rockabilly
Jerry Lee Lewis
Stray Cats

Pop, Rock, and Hard Rock
The Beatles
Jimi Hendrix
Eric Clapton
The Rolling Stones
Led Zeppelin
The Doors
Pink Floyd
Aerosmith
Van Halen
Guns N' Roses
Nirvana
Pearl Jam
Soundgarden

JAZZ
New Orleans Second Line
Olympia Brass Hall
Galactic

Dixieland
Louis Armstrong
Preservation Hall Jazz Band

Big Band
Duke Ellington
Gene Krupa
Count Basie
Glenn Miller
Buddy Rich
Brian Setzer

Small Group Jazz
Charlie Parker
John Coltrane
Miles Davis
Thelonious Monk

BLUES
John Lee Hooker
T-Bone Walker
B.B. King
Stevie Ray Vaughan

FUNK
New Orleans Funk
The Meters
Dr. John
The Neville Brothers

"Grease" Funk (ghost notes)
James Brown
Average White Band
Parliament
Tower of Power

Funk Rock

Sly & the Family Stone
Ohio Players
Stevie Wonder
Earth, Wind & Fire
Kool & the Gang
Red Hot Chili Peppers
Dave Matthews Band

Hip-Hop/Rap

The Sugarhill Gang
MC Hammer
N.W.A.
Dr. Dre
Snoop Dogg

Disco

Saturday Night Fever soundtrack
KC and the Sunshine Band
ABBA
Bee Gees

COUNTRY
Western Swing

Bob Wills

Honky Tonk

Hank Williams
Waylon Jennings

Outlaw Country

Johnny Cash
Willie Nelson

Country Rock

Eagles
Marshall Tucker Band

Traditional Country

Patsy Cline
Winona Judd

Present Day Bluegrass

Dixie Chicks

Modern Country

Garth Brooks
Rascal Flatts
Tim McGraw

LATIN
Bossa Nova

Antonio Carlos Jobim

Samba

Nana Vasconcelos
Airto Moreira
Sergio Mendes

Cha-Cha

Tito Puente

Soca

Mighty Sparrow

Calypso

Harry Belafonte

Mambo

Tito Puente
Machito

Songo

Michel Camilo
Eddie Palmieri

Kennan Wylie holds a Bachelors and Masters degree in Music Education from the University of North Texas. He was an adjunct professor of percussion at University of Arlington for ten years and is currently the percussion instructor at Marcus High School in Flower Mound, Texas. Under his direction since 1990, the Marcus group has received national acclaim both on and off the field. Kennan has authored several books geared toward the teaching of beginning percussion. He has presented clinics throughout the country as well as at the Percussive Arts Society International Convention (PASIC). He is also the past president of the Texas Percussive Arts Society. Wylie plays with the band Fingerprints from the Dallas/Ft. Worth area and is an active freelance musician. He is endorsed by Yamaha Drums, Evans Heads, Innovative Percussion, and Zildjian Cymbals.

Gregg Bissonette is one of the most versatile drummers in the business. Known for his wide range of styles and expertise, he has played with many of the world's leading musicians including Ringo Starr, David Lee Roth, James Taylor, Santana (on his Grammy-award winning album *Supernatural*), Don Henley, Joe Satriani, Andrea Bocelli, ELO, Maynard Ferguson, Spinal Tap, and countless others. He performs regularly in Ringo Starr's All Starr Band. Gregg has also recorded for many films—including *The Bucket List*, *Finding Nemo*, *Best in Show*, *For Your Consideration*, *The Bourne Supremacy*, *The Mighty Wind*, *The Polar Express*, *The Devil Wears Prada*, *Waiting for Guffman*, *Forgetting Sarah Marshall*, *The 40-Year-Old Virgin*—and TV shows, including the hit NBC series *Friends*. He is endorsed by Dixon Drums, Sabian Cymbals, DW, Samson, Remo, Vic Firth, and LP.

A very special thanks to:

Joel McCray – creative audio composition

Bill Bachman – audio engineer

Robert Poole – engraving assistance